HOOVER SCHOOL
Wayne, MI.

This Book is Donated

by *Stephanie R. McKee*

1998-1999

If...

by Sarah Perry

The J. Paul Getty Museum *and* Children's Library Press

The J. Paul Getty Museum
17985 Pacific Coast Highway
Malibu, California 90265-5799

Children's Library Press
P.O. Box 2609
Venice, California 90294

At the J. Paul Getty Museum:
Christopher Hudson, Publisher
Mark Greenberg, Managing Editor
John Harris, Editor

At J. Paul Getty Trust Publication Services:
Suzanne Watson Petralli, Production Coordinator

At Children's Library Press:
Jerry Sohn, Publisher
Teresa Bjornson, Editor in Chief

Separations by Heinz Weber, Inc., Los Angeles, California
Printed and bound by Tien Wah Press, Singapore

Library of Congress Cataloging-in-Publication Data

Perry, Sarah
  If... / Sarah Perry.
    p. cm.
    Summary: Illustrations present such imaginative possibilities as
worms with wheels, caterpillar toothpaste, and whales in outer space.
    ISBN 0-89236-321-5
    [1. Imagination—Fiction] I. Title
PZ7.P43595If 1995
[E]—dc20   94-35108
                  CIP
                  AC

10 9 8 7 6 5 4 3 2

If cats could fly...

If mice were hair...

If worms had wheels...

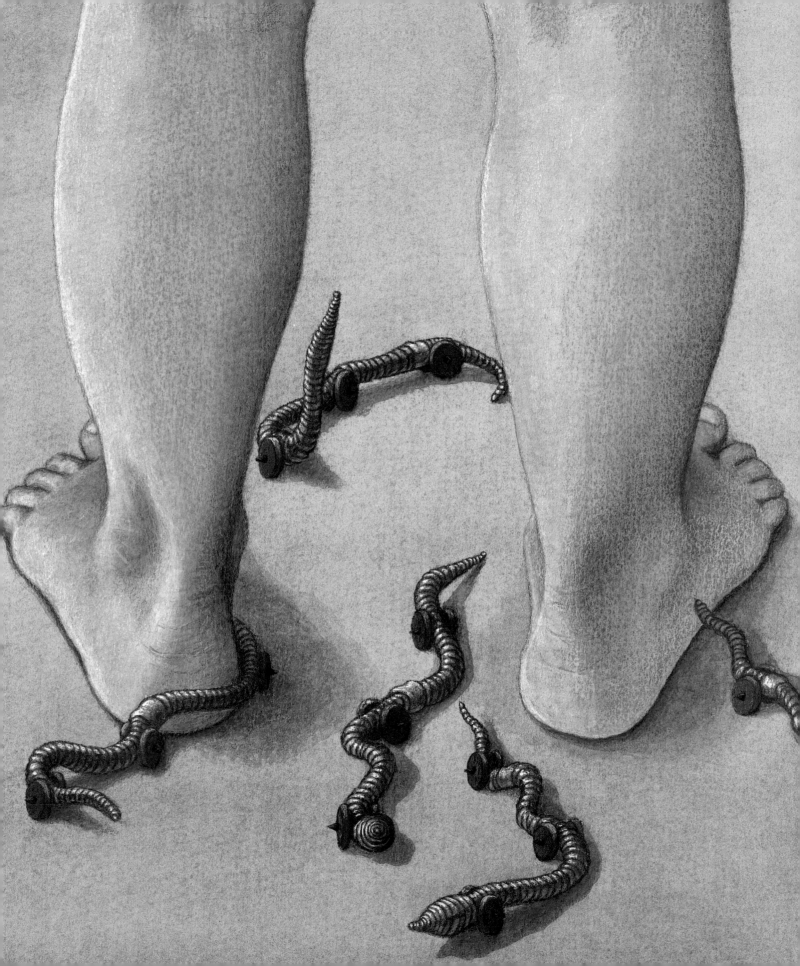

If frogs ate rainbows...

If dogs were mountains...

If zebras had stars and stripes...

If music could be held...

If ugly were beautiful...

If toes were teeth...

If caterpillars were toothpaste...

If whales lived in outer space...

If leaves were fish...

If clouds were spirits...

If butterflies were clothes...

If lightning made rhinos...

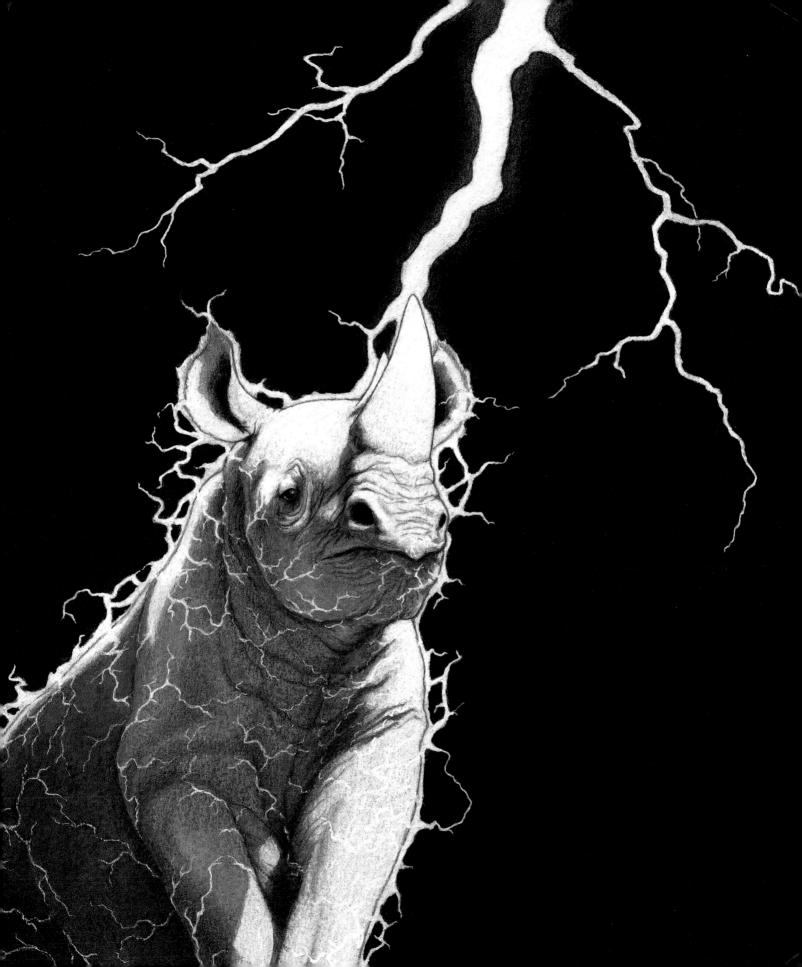

If ants could count...

If the moon were square...

If kids had tails...

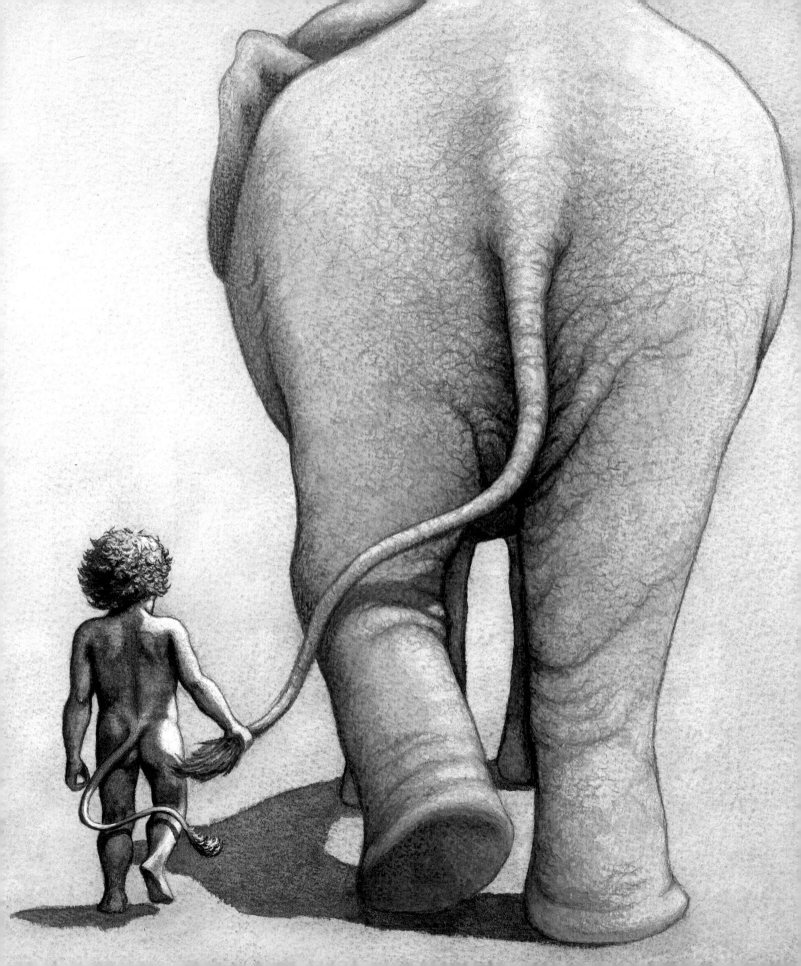

If spiders could read braille...

If hummingbirds told secrets...

If this is the end...

Then dream up some more!